gage

Canadian
First Book of
WORDS

Senior Consultant
Ron Benson

gagelearning

© 2002   Gage Learning Corporation
164 Commander Blvd., Toronto, ON M1S 3C7
www.gagelearning.com

Illustrations: The Macquarie Library Pty Ltd ©1998

We acknowledge the financial support of the Government of Canada through the Book Publishing Industry Development Program for our publishing activities.

We wish to thank the following educators for their advice and assistance: Stephen Dow and Kathryn Mattison

National Library of Canada Cataloguing in Publication Data

Main entry under title: The Gage Canadian first book of words (Gage Canadian reference series)

ISBN 0-7715-2010-7

1. English language—Dictionaries, Juvenile. I. Title. II. Series.

PE1628.5.G324 2002   j423   C2002-900605-8

Design and additional illustrations: ArtPlus Limited
ISBN **0-7715-2010-7**

1 2 3 4 5 GG 06 05 04 03 02

Written, printed, and bound in Canada

GAGE CANADIAN REFERENCE SERIES

Gage Canadian Dictionary
Gage Canadian Thesaurus
Gage Canadian Concise Dictionary
Gage Canadian Writer's Handbook

Gage Canadian Intermediate Dictionary
Gage Canadian Student Writer's Guide

Gage Canadian Junior Dictionary
Gage Canadian School Dictionary
Gage Canadian School Thesaurus
Gage Canadian Writers in Action Handbook

Gage Canadian Beginner's Dictionary
Gage Canadian First Book of Words

Contents

Off to a Great Start

ambulance

The *Gage Canadian First Book of Words* has two primary uses:

➤ **as a source of word meanings**
The pictures and accompanying labels combine to provide a word definition.

➤ **as a resource for conventional spelling**
The *Gage Canadian First Book of Words* provides children with the conventional spelling of a storehouse of the most-requested words. In this book, children will find the first 300 most common words in the English language, as reflected in the *Gage Canadian Spelling* Series and *The Reading Teacher's Book of Lists*. These words make up about 65 percent of all written material. The Appendix holds a collection of theme words: days of the week, parts of the body, and so on. In total, there are nearly 600 words for children to look at, to talk about, to "play with," to build into their vocabulary, to learn to read, and to enjoy.

Activities and Exercises

This section is for those teachers, parents, or other adults who will be using the *Gage Canadian First Book of Words* with a child or group of children, in a school or home setting. Several of the activities can be used in situations with one child, with a pair or small group of children, or with a large group. For easier reading, we have used the word *children* to mean an individual child, a small group of children, or a class of children.

The following is a selection of activities to introduce and reinforce various dictionary skills such as recognizing the various alphabet letters and securing their position. The activities are grouped according to the nature of their word focus rather than in order from easier to more difficult. You will be able to select those tasks that best suit the abilities, skills, and current learning needs of the particular individual or group of children you're working with.

Begin by taking the children on a walk through the book, stopping along the way to notice its outstanding features:

• the picture on the cover
• the large alphabet letters at the top of each left-hand page
• the colourful visuals
• the word collections
• the page numbers
• the alphabetical order

To encourage the children's participation, you could ask:
What do you see on this page? Do you see . . .? What do you notice about . . .?

Using the Left-Hand Pages

I Spy This exercise helps the children to discriminate between words, using a variety of characteristics. Use the Aa page as an example.

Say: I spy with my little eye **(pause briefly so the children have time to focus on the entire page)** something that begins with the letter *a* **(as a letter name reinforcement)** and is good to eat **(apple)**.

Say: I spy with my little eye **(pause)** something that can move **(pause so the children can begin to discriminate)** that has wheels and that takes sick people to the hospital **(ambulance)**. I spy with my little eye **(pause)** a word that has three letters **(children will now be looking at *axe* and *ant* and waiting for the next clue)** that is black and has legs **(ant)**.

Spell the Word This exercise lets the children practise letter recognition. Use the Bb page as an example.

Ask: Who can spell the word that names a fruit that's good to eat? **(b-a-n-a-n-a)**

Say: That's right, b-a-n-a-n-a. A banana is a fruit that's good to eat. **(You are thus reinforcing the spelling, the word, and the word meaning.)**

Point to the Picture This activity helps the children to discriminate between and among pictures and to reinforce word meanings. Use the Cc page as an example.

Say: Point to the picture of something that a mouse likes to eat **(cheese)** has a face **(clock or camel)** walks on four legs **(camel)** has two hands **(clock)**.

Point to the Letter This activity helps the children to reinforce the concept of letter and the letter names. Use the Dd page as an example.

Say: Point to the picture of the dentist. Put your finger on the word *dentist*. Point to each letter as I say its name d-e-n-t-i-s-t.

As you give each instruction and as you say each letter name, check to be certain the children are pointing to the correct response.

Using the Right-Hand Pages

The word lists on the right-hand pages offer an opportunity for the children to notice how a word list differs from the format of print in a story.

Count Them Up! To reinforce the format and to establish that these pages are ordered in vertical columns, have the children count the words in the list beginning top left, moving vertically down the page, and then go to the top of the second column.

Look, Point, and Follow Along The children aren't expected to be able to read the words; however, this experience will allow you to monitor the children to see if they can track top to bottom, then go to the top of the second column. Use the Ll page as an example. Read the list of words aloud, beginning with *last* and ending with *love*, while the children point to the words.

Spell the Picture On several pages there is an illustration without a printed word to accompany it.

Use the Gg page as an example. Have the children look for and identify the wordless picture (goat). Invite the children to try to spell the word *goat*. Record their attempts on chart paper or the chalkboard.

Rhyme the Words This activity helps the children to reinforce initial consonants.

Several of the words in the lists can be used as springboards to rhyme, for example, *back* (sack, Jack, pack, track), or *like* (bike, hike, Mike). Print the source word on chart paper, the chalkboard, or a magic slate and invite the children to think of a word that rhymes. Suggest what letter (perhaps *s*) the new word would start with. It's important for the children to understand that it's sound and not spelling that determines words that "rhyme."

Make a Word Children can make new words by adding an initial consonant to the beginning of some of the words. Use the Aa page: *and* (band, hand, land, sand)

Take a Guess This activity helps to anchor the sound of selected initial consonants in the ears of the children, and lets them focus on word meanings.

The initial consonants *m*, *r*, *s*, and *v* often provide the best initial choice because, unlike the other consonants, their sounds can be sustained (mmmmmmmmm, rrrrrrrrrrrrrrrrrrr, sssssssssssssssss, vvvvvvvvvvvvvv) so the children can hear them more easily.

Make a Copy This activity helps children to copy accurately.

Children will enjoy choosing a word (or words) to copy. They could use Plasticine, sand, or paint to print the words. For words that they can read, the children could print the word and then use crayons to make a picture that explains the word's meaning through a visual context.

Sing the Alphabet Song To give the children practice finding various letter pages, sing the alphabet song to them and stop at various letters at which time the children can search for and locate a page that corresponds to the letter you stopped at.

ABCDEFG
HIJKLMNOP
QRSTUV
W XYZ

Sing the alphabet song together as you point to a posted alphabet chart. To help anchor the letter's location, always start singing from the beginning of the alphabet — the children will hear that, for example, *C* is near the beginning, *M* is near the middle and *Y* is near the end.

Aa

ambulance

ant

apple

axe

b
c
d
e
f
g
h
i
j
k
l
m
n
o
p
q
r
s
t
u
v
w
x
y
z

above	always
add	and
address	animal
after	answer
again	any
air	ask
all	away
almost	
alone	
also	

Bb

balloon

banana

beaver

bee

back   big

ball   bike

because   bird

before   birthday

begin   book

behind   both

below   box

best   boy

better

between

a
b
c
d
e
f
g
h
i
j
k
l
m
n
o
p
q
r
s
t
u
v
w
x
y
z

Cc

camel

Canada

cheese

clock

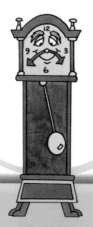

call

can

car

carefully

carry

cat

chair

children

class

close

clothes

cloud

cold

colour

come

computer

country

crayon

cut

Dd

dentist

dinosaur

dog

dragon

dad	don't
dark	down
date	draw
day	dream
deep	dress
dish	drink
do	drop
doctor	dry
doesn't	
done	

Ee

ear

egg

elephant

eye

early	even
easy	ever
eat	everybody
e-mail	excellent
empty	exciting
end	exit
engine	expect
enjoy	
equal	

Ff

fire truck

flag

fork

frog

face	floor
family	flower
far	food
farm	for
fast	found
father	friend
favourite	from
find	front
first	fun
fish	

Gg

gift

giraffe

glove

goose

game

garden

gave

get

girl

give

glad

go

gold

gone

good

goodbye

got

grass

great

ground

grow

guess

Hh

hammer

helmet

hockey stick

horse

had	hear
hair	help
hamburger	high
hand	home
happy	hot
hard	house
has	how
have	
head	

I i

iceberg

ice cream

insect

island

ice	inside
icing	Internet
idea	is
if	it
ill	its
I'll	it's
in	itself

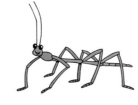

a b c d e f g h i j k l m n o p q r s t u v w x y z

A
B
C
D
E
F
G
H
I
J
K
L
M
N
O
P
Q
R
S
T
U
V
W
X
Y
Z

Jj

jam

jar

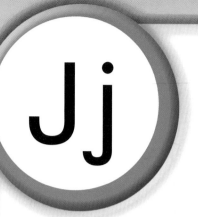

jigsaw

juice

jacket

jeans

jello

jelly bean

job

join

joke

jumbo

jump

jungle

just

Kk

kangaroo

kayak

kite

kitten

karate	kind
keep	king
key	knife
keyboard	know
kick	

Ll

ladder

leaf

lid

lobster

last	line
laugh	lion
leave	list
left	little
let	live
letter	long
library	lose
lift	lost
light	love
like	

Mm

magnet

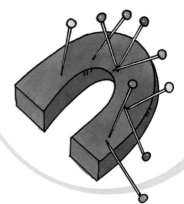

mask

monkey

mouse

machine	money
made	moon
make	more
man	morning
many	most
may	mother
meet	move
milk	much
minute	mud
mom	

Nn

nail

nest

nose

nut

name	nobody
near	noise
neat	north
need	not
never	note
new	nothing
next	now
night	number

a b c d e f g h i j k l m n o p q r s t u v w x y z

A B C D E F G H I J K L M N O P Q R S T U V W X Y Z

Oo

octopus

open

orange

owl

of	or
off	other
office	our
often	out
oh	outside
old	over
on	own
once	
only	

Pp

paint

pelican

pig

puppet

pair	plane
paper	play
parents	please
park	present
party	pretend
pencil	pull
pet	push
phone	put
picture	puzzle
piece	

Qq

quack

quarter

queen

quilt

question

quick

quiet

quit

quite

quiz

Rr

rabbit

rainbow

refrigerator

rocket

race	road
rain	rock
reach	roll
read	room
real	rose
really	round
remember	row
rest	run
right	
river	

a b c d e f g h i j k l m n o p q r s t u v w x y z

Ss

scissors

seagull

shark

spider

say   sit

school   sleep

second   small

see   smile

shape   snow

shoe   soft

short   sort

show   sound

sign   story

sing

a b c d e f g h i j k l m n o p q r s t u v w x y z

T t

taxi

tiger

tooth

train

tail	today
take	tomorrow
talk	top
teacher	touch
television	tree
thick	trick
thin	truck
thing	try
think	turn
time	

Uu

umbrella

underwear

uniform

universe

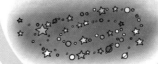

ugly   upside down

under   us

unless   use

until   usually

up

Vv

vacuum cleaner

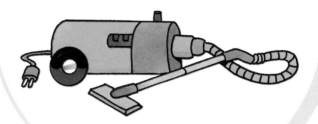

vase

vegetable

volcano

van   view

very   visit

vet   voice

video

a
b
c
d
e
f
g
h
i
j
k
l
m
n
o
p
q
r
s
t
u
v
w
x
y
z

Ww

web

wheel

winter

worm

wall	which
want	wish
warm	with
was	without
water	woman
wave	word
week	work
well	world
went	wrong
where	

X x

X ray

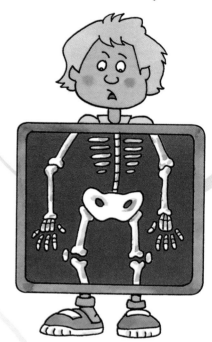

xylophone

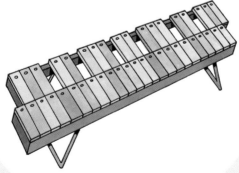

x's and o's

Y y

yacht

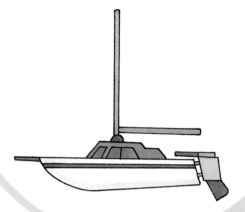

yellow

yolk

yo-yo

yard	yet
yawn	you
year	young
yell	your
yes	you're
yesterday	yourself

Zz

zebra

zero

5 4 3 2 1 0

zipper

zoo

zap

zigzag

zone

Colours

black

orange

blue

purple

brown

red

green

white

grey

yellow

Shapes and Solids

Shapes

triangle

rectangle

square

diamond

circle

Solids

cone

cylinder

sphere

pyramid

cube

Numbers and Coins

1	one
2	two
3	three
4	four
5	five
6	six
7	seven
8	eight
9	nine
10	ten
100	one hundred
1000	one thousand
1 000 000	one million

 cent

 nickel

 dime

 quarter

 loonie

 toonie

Days, Months, and Seasons

Days

Monday
Tuesday
Wednesday
Thursday
Friday
Saturday
Sunday

Months

January
February
March
April
May
June
July
August
September
October
November
December

Seasons

Spring
Summer
Fall or Autumn
Winter

The Body

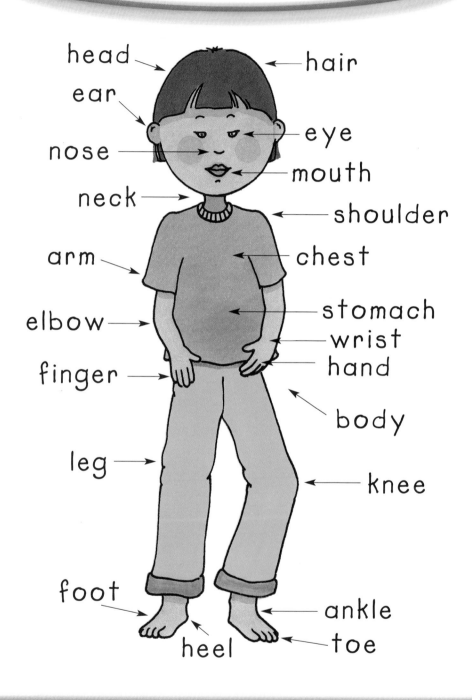

head — hair

ear

nose — eye

mouth

neck — shoulder

arm — chest

elbow — stomach
wrist
hand

finger

body

leg — knee

foot

heel — ankle
toe